The three magic keys
&
Laura of Calabazas

Rita Mendoza

THE THREE MAGIC KEYS
&
LAURA OF CALABAZAS

Illustrated by

EMELY FERNÁNDEZ

New Jersey
United State of America
2019

Copyright

This book is registered in the National Copyright Office (ONDA), in the Dominican Republic under number 04253/08/17. Reproductions in any form such as electronic, manual, photocopy or audio, without the written approval of the author, is prohibited according to Art. 57 and 58 of the regulations of application of law 65-00 No.362 -01 of 14 of March 14, 2001.

ISBN 978-164713237-8

Printed by H & L Printing
343 Boulevard Suites A
Hasbrouck Heights, NJ 07604,
United States
E-mail: hlprint@aol.com

This book is dedicated to all of those who have been and will be part of my life, to my relatives, friends and of course to my inseparable companion of adventures, my beloved Brownie.

I am infinitely grateful to an extraordinary person who inspired the character of Arkazú. Through him, I learned to trust and believe that there are noble people who come to our lives in the least expected moment to fill us with light and love.

I hope that everyone who reads this book can find *"The Three Magic Keys"* and with them open the doors of a better world.

Rita Mendoza

I want to give a very special thanks to my niece and illustrator of this story, Emely Fernandez who at thirteen years of age has great talent and creativity. I know that like her, other girls of her age will identify with the values and teachings that this book contains.

The three magic keys

In a village in the distant kingdom of Arabella, a girl with a very strange appearance was born. She was so different that she completely changed the lives of all the people; living in the small and humble village of Calabazas. Laura, as the girl was named, was very sweet, playful and as naughty as hare.

Her face was very peculiar, with big, bright eyes that shone like stars, ears protruding from her wavy brown hair and a heart-shaped mole on each of her cheeks made the little girl exceptional among the people of Calabazas and the entire kingdom of Arabella.

Despite her remarkable differences, the inhabitants of Calabazas adored her. It was a delight for them to spend time with her; they would take her to the forest where they harvested vegetables and fruits for nourishment. Among the harvest were pumpkins, from which the name of the village arose. They prepared delicious creams, soups, and desserts with the cavity of the pumpkin and used its exterior to make the lamps that illuminated the quiet and happy village of Calabazas every night.

The three magic keys

Every day was the same routine, the villagers got up very early in the morning to plant in the fields. Their work was accompanied by the melodious chirping of the hummingbirds. The beautiful melody could be heard everywhere. Women would go to the river every morning to fetch water for the animals to drink. They were also in charge of preparing food for their families.

Laura was happy and cheerful little girl. She learned to play the bamboo flute, an instrument that the good and blind Bartolomeo made for her with his bare hands. Although he had been blind since birth, the sensation of touch, the anatomy of the instrument against his fingers, more than compensated for the loss of sight.

In the Calabazas Village, there were no schools and families were so poor; that they could not afford to send their children to neighboring village schools. Therefore, every villager was responsible for teaching their trades or skills to all the children in the village. Including Diego, who didn't have the ability to hear and was communicated to with the use of sign language.

Mrs. Serafina was responsible for teaching them to read and write. As a young girl her parents sent her to the village of Solgiral, where she nursed and care for the children of a noble family.

Rita Mendoza

However, she took advantage of the classes the children received and applied everything that she had learned in secret. Thanks to her resourcefulness everyone in the village learned to count, read and write correctly.

Rigoberto and his wife Lucia couldn't have children, so they tended to the needs of children in the village as well. Lucia enjoyed preparing pumpkin desserts every afternoon and giving them to the apprentices of her husband Rigoberto. The children adored her as well as Rigoberto or "Grumble" as they called him.

The seamstress Carmelia taught the young girls, including Laura, how to sow buttons and mend clothes. Carmelia explained that the more things they learned, the more opportunities they will have in life.

Mrs. Gervasia, on the other hand, transmitted her love for flowers. She taught the children about the meaning of each of them and their colors and how plants were like people. "They can feel and hear what we tell them. People should treat them with respect and give them a lot of love; so that in return there can be beautiful and perfumed flowers throughout the year".

Another of the many things that the young people learned was about the properties of herbs and spices. A master of such a topic was Maravides, who learned everything about them from his grandfather. Maravides revealed the miracles of the ointments and infusions to alleviate all kinds of affections and ailments.

In his small garden, Maravides had aloe plants, which were said to be useful for everything. They healed wounds and burns, grew hair, make skin softer, and could be taken to relieve stomach problems. In short, they were believed to be very beneficial, even in warding off bad energies.

In his garden were mint plants, good herb, rosemary, chamomile and lavender which he used to prepare delicious teas. Also there were other aromatic species which he used in the preparation of perfumes that he sold in the "big city" as it was called in the kingdom of Arabella.

Grandpa Enrique, as all the children in Calabazas called Laura's grandfather, enjoyed telling his stories about the great city, the palace of king Amadeus, the sea and everything that live there, all the things and people he met while working in the royal palace. The were fascinated with all the places that were mentioned to the point of dreaming they might visit them one day.

The village artist was the prodigious Mr. Rafaelo, who was known and admired for his extraordinary works. He drew and painted pictures, portraits and created sculptures of all kinds. Rafaelo was in charge of teaching children to paint and mix colors.

With his guidance they learned to make figures with the resin of the trees and to extract the pigment from vegetables; such as mint, beets, raspberries, blueberries, carrots and many others; they also used the colors of spices like saffron, turmeric and minerals such as: coal, clay and fruits in particular cocoa and coffee.

The villagers could not afford to buy expensive paint to beautify their houses. Rafaelo and other young people were in charge of giving color to the village. Each house and each corner told its own story.

It was very easy to identify the home of each person because they painted it according to their skills or personality. For example: the wooden walls of Gervasia house was painted with the flowers, which she loved because they were reflection of her beautiful garden. Bartolomeo, being a musician chose to decorate his home with of portraits and musical notes coming out of a bamboo flute.

At the house of the grumpy Rigoberto, you could find a huge shoe and beside it, the delicious pumpkin dessert made by his wife. Rafaelo was very patient with the children, especially with Laura who always asked him to create a portrait of her. His heart broke into pieces, because he was not able to please her. Everyone in the village agreed to prevent her from seeing her own face. He always made up an excuse so that she wouldn't feel sad. That was the way of life in the little town of Calabazas; everyone contributed and shared their knowledge with others. They were very united and generous people.

In the kingdom of Arabella, it was customary by law to choose nine girls every year to represent their villages in the big city. The villages were as fallow: Pan de Frutas, Solgiral, Damasco, Carambolas, Champiñon, Los Lírios, Flamboyán, Uveral and Monte Verde, apart from Calabazas.

The kingdom was preparing for the great royal banquet; which was the perfect opportunity for the young girls to present their village's requests to the King. In order for him to grant a royal shield, which symbolizes his desire to help the villages.

In Calabazas a very precarious situation arose. The number of inhabitants had increased drastically and the food was scarce due to the lack of land for planting in recent years. For the first time in a long time, they had to resort to the help of king Amadeus.

Everyone in the village wondered who could go to the big city to represent them. Even though, none of the girls were prepared for such a long journey, or to appear in front of the King. Laura bravely decided to go, in search of help for her village, which was desperately needed.

Before appearing in front of the King, the girls had to attend an etiquette and protocol school for ladies. In which they were taught how to behave properly and learn a trade which they would teach their families and others in their villages. It was similar to the way Laura and other children learned from all the villagers in Calabazas.

In spite of how happy Laura's parents and all the villagers of Calabazas were when they saw her go in search of help; they kept worrying about the difficulties that she could face, because she was so different from the other girls with whom she would attend school. Their hearts clenched with sadness and fear, as they knew it was a very difficult mission, knowing that not even the most beautiful young girl of their humble village could obtain the much desired royal shield.

Laura was very happy, dreaming of the wonderful future that awaited her, her parents and all the villagers of their beloved Calabazas. Whom with all their love built a wagon with pieces of old wood found in the forest. Laura went to the big city; accompanied by a weak donkey called Molondrón, a name he got from a vegetable grown in the village.

Although Molondrón needed strength, little by little he pulled the screeching cart; Meanwhile, Laura thought about all the new things she was going to learn and see in the big city. However, she never thought about how different she was from others, because in her village everyone loved her and never made her feel different.

On the way, Laura could see the large and leafy trees in an endless meadows ideal for rabbits that jumped and played everywhere. As well as the multicolored butterflies fluttering around, she saw the hummingbirds extracting the sweet nectar from the roses and she also could smell the perfume of the flowers in the air, as the river babbled and birds chirped. It was a magical experience for her!

As the night came, Laura stopped to rest under a gigantic tree where she spread the blanket that her mother gave her. Azucena started to weave that blanket when Laura was a child. Azucena bought a roll of wool whenever she could in order to finish the blanket. Although she took a long time, she finished just in time for the departure of the innocent young girl.

The night was warm and the sky was covered by a veil of stars, revealing a huge and radiant moon. Molondrón, the fireflies and the chirping crickets were Laura's only company.

Between deep sighs, Laura looked at the stars and began to think that perhaps one day she could shine as brilliantly as one of them. Her deep thoughts were interrupted by the braying of her donkey who was hungry. He had spent all day without eating like Laura, who did not have enough food to sustain them on the long journey. She thought she had carefully divided the fruits and vegetables given by the villagers so that they would last until arriving at her destination.

She fed Molondrón and then gazed at the sky, observed a shooting star that illuminates the heavens. She made a wish abruptly, which brought back memories; of when her grandfather took her to the mountain top to see the stars. Her grandfather had told her that if she ever saw a shooting star she should not forget to make a wish. Also if she made a wish with all her heart, it would become a reality.

Deeply exhausted from the journey, Laura and Molondrón fell asleep. The next day, the bright light from the sun and the chirping of birds woke her up. She hurriedly washed her face and brush her teeth, then folds her blanket and continued her journey. In order for her to be accepted into school she had to arrive at her destination on the third day, if not she would disappoint the villagers who loved and trusted her.

Laura had a voice as beautiful as the fairies and loved by everyone who heard it. While on the road, her singing attracted the attention of birds, butterflies, hares and all the animals of the forest. They all were delighted to hear her sing. In a distance, she could see the reflection of a village and could hear the hubbub of people moving from one place to another.

As she got closer and closer, the scent of smoke from a chimney saturated the air. She closed her eyes with a sigh and inhaled the blackberries and strawberries that made her lips savor. Unable to contain the smell of such lovely delicacies, she followed the scent until it led her to the location it had come from.

She arrived at the village Pan de Frutas, which, like all the other villages in Arabella's kingdom, acquired the name of the flowers, fruits or food they prepared.

Within this village were the most delicious desserts and fruit cakes were found. Every morning the atmosphere was soaked with their smells. Eager to try even a bit of the delightful cakes, Laura went into the village; without imagining the reaction of the villagers to her. Several of them stopped their work in order to listen where the strange noise was coming from.

Laura's cart was so old that it made such terrible noise. The wheels wobbled and the wood creaked as if it was falling apart. The villagers were astonished; they could not believe what they saw.

Everyone stood still and were amazed watching the wagon pass by. It was not the old ramshackle cart that took their breath away, it was her peculiarity. The innocent young girl of Calabazas greeted everyone in the Pan de Frutas with a smile, without noticing how astonished they were as they looked at her.

That was when everything began. The people were silent; no one dared to say a single word or smile back. Until a child who was in his mother's arms, looked at the young girl and with his little fingers pointed, said "Mommy, look how weird and ugly that girl look!"

Rita Mendoza

Upon hearing the words of the child, everyone began to laugh and make fun of the young girl who was unaware of her appearance. They said that she was the most horrible creature they had ever seen. The sweet and innocent village girl of Calabazas began to cry and ran as fast as she could to the old cart; forcing Molondrón to speed.

Fortunately, she walked away from Pan de Frutas, unable to believe the cruelty of those people she encountered. She had never been treated like that before, so it was difficult to understand why they called her a strange ugly creature.

Laura had never seen her face. The day that she was born her parents and other villagers of Calabazas destroyed all the mirrors in the village so she could never see herself and feels different. She was never allowed to fetch water at the river for the same reason. Laura never knew the secret carefully guarded by those who loved her so much.

When arriving at the top of a mountain, Laura and Molondrón stopped to spend the night. They had to rest in order to arrive on time within the great city the following day.

Rejected and saddened by the jokes of the villagers of Pan de Frutas, she found refuge in a cave. While in the cave she observed the stars, but their brightness was overshadowed by the tears that profusely flowed from her eyes. She asked herself why had the people been so cruel and what could be so strange about her? She believed that she looked the same as all the villagers in Calabazas; in fact the villagers had told her that she was the most beautiful girl in the whole village.

They believed she was the most beautiful because they saw the beauty of her heart. Laura was very noble and she cared for all people and for the animals so that they could be happy. She entertained them and made them laugh, embraced them with hugs and kisses and delighted them with her melodious voice.

The people from her village considered her traits as genuinely beautiful; the type of beauty that comes from within. They knew that there were people who look very beautiful on the exterior, yet who could be quiet evil and cruel on the inside and that Laura was about to discover this fact. Sobbing and without anyone to comfort her, she fell asleep.

The next morning the braying of Molondrón woke her up. She had not realized the sun had already risen because she was in cave. When she realized the time, she took her things and ran out to the cart.

It was late and she had a long journey ahead. She had to arrive before sunset, otherwise all her effort would be in vain. The speed was too much causing a wheel of the cart to be break, on a stone path. She thought that she had missed her opportunity and disappointed all who trusted her. She believed the villagers would never be granted the royal shield and Calabazas would not be favored by the King.

Suddenly, she heard someone approaching; it was an old man with his oxen who plowed the land for planting of crops. When he saw her, he went to help her. However, she was afraid that he would bully her as the people of Pan de Frutas had, so she hid from him.

The old man said, "Do not be afraid, I just want to help fix your cart;" and Laura replied, "I appreciate your generosity, but I do not want you to see my face. Although, I am the same as everyone, some people think otherwise and you probably will too". He will share the same unpleasant thoughts as the people of Pan de Frutas and as a result he will make fun of me, she believed.

The old man then told her that he could never make fun of her since he sees beyond physical features. He could see the hearts of people and hers was full of kindness.

Rita Mendoza

Upon hearing his reassuring words she revealed herself to him. The old man named Arkazú looked at her and said; she didn't have to be ashamed because she was a very special and beautiful person. While repairing the cart they talked about the reasons that led her to that place.

Arkazú was a very wise man; he immediately knew Laura's motives and advised her the way her grandfather would. He told her the dangers and difficulties she could face while trying to acquire the royal shield. He also spoke about the values of life, things more precious than physical beauty and couldn't be bought with money that could only be possessed by people with pure and noble hearts.

Laura was captivated by the description of such could values and why they were so priceless. After he finished repairing the cart, the wise Arkazú give the young lady a gift.

Arkazú gave her three golden keys. Each of them represented a different value that when applied by Laura would make them shine. He asked that she always keep them with her, but especially during difficult times.

He also told her that it didn't matter what other people thought about her. The three keys would give her the strength to succeed in life and make her dreams come true. Laura embraced the wise Arkazú with a hug, promised she would visit him on her return to Calabazas and said goodbye.

She stored the valuable keys very well and proceeded happily to her destiny. She arrived just before sunset and entered through a big golden door that protected the city. Her eyes popped and her smile broadened because of how stunned she was with everything she saw.

The houses of the big city had huge doors with bright colors. The streets were full of people and merchants, from all the neighboring kingdoms. They came there to sell their products which include fine fabrics, precious stones, gold, silver and copper threads, all kinds of crafts and antiques. There was also a great variety of fruits, vegetables, flowers, and spices.

The richest men and women in Arabella dressed in very elegant garments that were often lined with gold embroidery and ornaments with pearls, sapphires, and rubies. The aroma of the city was provided by perfumes made from roses.

Everything seemed lovely to Laura. She couldn't believe that there was so much wealth in Arabella, in comparison to the villagers of Calabazas, who barely had anything to eat; even though, they were in charge of harvesting their food. They had to sell a portion of the crops to pay taxes to the King and shared what remained amongst themselves. The villagers were very poor and could not afford to wear fine and expensive fabrics or beautiful stones, unlike those in Arabella.

Another thing that made Calabazas different from other villages was the people who lived there. They were good and kind people who helped each other and shared everything they had. They never tried to take advantage of their fellow villagers.

In the big city, the people were ecstatic about their wealth that they did not notice the old cart that roamed the streets of the kingdom, making a terrible noise and much less the strange young girl. Laura went on her way unnoticed, until she reached the place where she would begin to work for her village's future.

The representatives from other villagers had already arrived at the school; they too like Laura travelled a long way in search of the royal shield for their villages. Laura's presence created a commotion and they all began to mumble among themselves.

Laura approached one of the girls and tried to be friendly but was ignored, soon after, the other girls moved away from her, as if she was carrying something contagious.

Laura was very sad with the rejections she received from her classmates. Especially, when it was time for all the young ladies to introduce themselves to their teachers and classmates. All of them including the teacher made funny jokes about Laura when it was her turn. They mocked her and wondered how a girl of her condition could attempt to study at the school.

They believed it was impossible that someone as strange as Laura would pass the rigorous tests. The tests that would allow her, to appear in front of the King and request the desired royal shield. She felt so humiliated that she wanted to disappear. Laura began to think she was insignificant.

They laughed at her relentlessly and no one would act in her defense. Dejected by the cruelty of the other young girls, Laura remembered the words of the wise Arkazú: "No matter what other think about you, inside you have everything you need, you just have to believe".

She also remembered the three keys that the wise Arkazú had given her. The word "Love" was engraved on the first of the three keys. She held it in her hands and her face lit up. Then she heard a sweet voice saying: "You are a special, unique and wonderful being. You must love yourself and never be ashamed of who you are and never forget that true beauty is inside your heart".

Upon hearing those words, Laura gathered strength and stood up in front of everyone. She straightened her head and proceeded to introduce herself and her village. She mentioned the goodness of the land, its leafy trees, the green meadows and the animals that live there, but above all she was vocal about the value of the people.

Little by little the laughter and mockery ended as Laura spoke from the heart. Her voice was sweet and melodious as she talked and they listened. She spoke at length about the beauty, resources and traditions of Calabazas and about each and every one in her villager.

She explained how good her parents were, how much love they had given to her and all the wonderful lessons they had taught her, the meaning of their names: Benjamin, meaning Jasmine and Azucena, which was the name of a flower. Her parents had known each other, since they were children. They played in the forest caught butterflies and fireflies and had a very happy childhood. Most importantly they knew that someday they would be together forever.

Rita Mendoza

Laura never knew that her mother had also once been chosen to pursue the royal shield; but fate intervened. Azucena had to leave for the big city like all the other young girls. The journey she had made was the same as Laura's, but when Azucena arrived at the village of Pan de Frutas she found a home where a lonely woman who everyone was afraid of lived. During the time Azucena was on the road, she passed in front of an apparently "abandoned" house; out of nowhere a mysterious woman appeared and greeted her with a very friendly tone and a pleasant smile. The woman name was Pandora who invited the innocent young villager of Calabazas to spend the night in her house.

Azucena was so innocent that she trusted the sweet appearance of Pandora and agreed to her proposal. At dinner time Pandora prepared a large banquet worthy of a king. Azucena had never seen so much food in all her life. The table had the most delicious delicacies and desserts she had never tasted.

As they were having dinner they talked charmingly about Calabazas and her journey to conquer the royal shield. After the long journey and dinner, Azucena went to sleep in the guest room that Pandora had arranged for her. She fell asleep instantly without imagining what was about to happen.

Rita Mendoza

At midnight, the sweet and young Pandora became a horrendous, old wrinkled woman, with huge warts everywhere. Some of her teeth were missing and those that remained, were stained and sharpened as her long black nails. Pandora made her way to the room where Azucena was sleeping. She approached her and recited some strange words that extracted Azucena's youthfulness and cursed her forever.

The next day Azucena woke up in another place far from Pandora's home. Everything had seemed like a dream. She tried to look for Pandora but it was all in vain. Her weakness was evident; her skin no longer had the freshness and softness as before. Azucena's hair no longer shone like the sun, but still she continued with the trip.

Before arriving to the big city she stopped with her donkey to get water from a stream. Suddenly, she saw the reflection of an old man in the water; which shocked her, he said, "Azucena, as beautiful as the flower, you must return to your village as soon as possible. If not you will die and Pandora's curse will spread throughout Calabazas."

Azucena replied that she could not return to her village. She had to reach the big city in pursuit of the royal shield, which her people desperately needed.

"I understand that you want the welfare of your people more than anything. However, if you do not return as I ordered you, there will be no hope, and the whole village will be in darkness. The woman you met was real. Pandora is an evil sorceress who has stolen the brightness of your youth. On your return you will find a young man with good feelings. He will help and protect you, and with him you will make a home. Then you will bring forth a daughter who will finish the trip you started," said the old man.

"Your daughter will be very special. So take good care of her and give her all your love. Nurture her confidence and teach her to smile. These things will give her the necessary strength to fight against the difficulties she will face," after that, the old man disappeared.

Azucena was very confused. She did not know whether to return to her village and disappoint the people or continue on her journey, to the big city. The villagers trusted her so much, but she did not want the old man prediction to come true since it would be worst for Calabazas to be in darkness

After meditating, she made a decision and with the remaining strength she initiated a trip back home. Upon reaching the outskirts of Calabazas, Azucena fell off the cart. Luckily, a young man who was planting pumpkins seeds was right there and gave her aid.

The man removed her hair that cover her face and immediately knew who she was. It was his beautiful and beloved Azucena, the same girl that he played as child and dreamt of marrying someday. He quickly assisted her on the cart and took her to the village. Everyone left their homes, to see what had happened. They called the wisest elders of Calabazas and looked for the most powerful herbs; with which they made a potion that would restore the young girl's life.

Enrique, who was Azucena's father, was in the royal palace organizing the banquet and did not see his daughter's arrival. He started to worry, since all the other young ladies from the school were already present. He knew that something bad had happened. Immediately, he asked permission from King Amadeus to leave and traveled to the village. He never returned to the royal palace, or to the big city.

Arriving at Calabazas, Enrique was reunited with his daughter, who had spent three days in a deep sleep. He and all the villagers joined hands and asked for a miracle for his daughter. Then Azucena woke up in-front of everyone that was heartbroken. No one had suspected that Pandora's curse, although it had been extinguished thanks to the strength of the villagers love, left a deep mark on her.

Laura was born. Her big ears and eyes were a sign of Pandora's curse. Regardless of her eyes and ears, the love of the people of Calabazas was so powerful that it manifested as heart-shaped moles on both her cheeks; the villagers loved and protected the girl. Even though, her mother had not been able to obtain the royal shield, she sacrificed for them and Laura was so kind that it was impossible not to love her.

After Laura finished her presentation everyone was touched. They could not believe a special person was behind that strange face. She would utter kindest and subtlest of words despite the teasing and insults that she received.

The teachers were surprised and they had no choice but to allow Laura to stay in school, although they doubted her ability to make it to the end. Some of the students who had rejected Laura earlier approached her wanting to learn from her eloquence and strength, many of them could never endure as much humiliation as Laura had to go through.

At the end of the introduction to school, each girl was guided to their room. The girls from the wealthiest families had the most spacious and luxurious rooms, while the other girls were left with accommodations that were much more modest.

Because Laura was from a very humble village, they gave her a room outside the main house, next to the establishment. She was used to the country life, sleeping under the stars and not having amenities. She did not care about where she would be asked to stay, all she cared about was returning to her beloved village carrying the royal shield.

The place was dirty, full of debris and cobwebs everywhere; it also had an unpleasant smell because the horses slept next to it. This didn't discourage Laura. She had already passed the first test guided by the advice of Arkazú and through relying on the use of the first key, "***Love***".

Very early in the morning, before they all woke up, Laura looked for a broom and a bucket of water to clean the whole place. She removed the cobwebs, dusted and swept every corner and took out everything that did not work. It was not a difficult task for her, since she was a little girl she helped with household chores. Laura placed some wildflowers in a bowl of higüero that had been cut from the garden and accommodated the narrow bed with the blanket that her mother had woven.

Rita Mendoza

She organized all the gifts the villagers from Calabazas gave her. She did not forget the three keys that Arkazú had given her. Before the sun came up, the small room was bright and despite the annoying smell of the horses, a delicate aroma emerged from the bowl of flowers.

After cleaning the small room, she took a bath and put on a pretty dress with flower embroidery, which was made especially for her by Carmelia. The seamstress, Carmelia, taught Laura how to knit and sew. The dresses, as well as many other gifts, were among the possessions the villagers had generously given to Laura for her stay in the big city.

Like Carmelia, Maravides prepared a perfume for Laura composed of lavender, ylang-ylang, orange blossom, lilac, geraniums and gardenias. Each ingredient was carefully measured in order to assure the creation of a refined aroma which no one, not even the richest women of all Arabella owned. Maravides also gave her a pink colored balm to highlight her lips and beautiful smile. With these accessories the young girl was ready for the first day of classes.

She left her small room and went to the house of studies. It was here she would once again meet with all the other young girls as well as the teachers. She was anxious but very excited about everything that she would learn soon. When she arrived at the hall they had already assembled, the students wearing dresses made of fine fabrics, precious jewels, lace headdresses and flowers in their hair. Berarminia, the most petulant of all, approached Laura and dropped a silk handkerchief to the floor ordered her to pick it up as if Laura was her servant.

Everyone started, including the teachers who did not say anything to defend Laura, but with a humility that often characterized her, she bent down and picked up the handkerchief, delicately folded it and with a big smile handed it to Berarminia, who enjoyed humiliating those less fortunate.

This was not all; Laura told her a few words that Berarminia would never forget, "The humble do not always bow, to the presumptuous, because of their shortcomings, they do it because of a greatness and nobility that resides within their heart."

Laura raised her head and went to her seat. Berarminia was stunned because she didn't achieve her objective, which was to ridicule Laura. On the contrary, she awoke the admiration of the other students for the young girl.

Rita Mendoza

Following the encounter, it was time for the first lesson, which would be taught by Clotilde, a robust woman with a military appearance, low tolerance level, and very strict with her Etiquette and Protocol class. She had a broad knowledge of both subject since she was very familiar with how the girls should behave in front of the King.

Clotilde explained everything they needed to learn before presenting themselves in front of the King. She would teach them about the appropriate behavior in any scenario they would encounter, how to properly sit, table manners, elocution As Clotilde was talking, Laura thought about her village; the people she left, the animals, the plants but especially her parents, suddenly she was interrupted from her wistfulness by Clotilde hitting the table with a ruler..

Laura jumped out of her seat and everyone laughed, which the teacher didn't approve of. Clotilde decide she would test Laura and at last be rid of her. From the first time she saw Laura she did not like her at all and thought it was a waste of time for her to attend the school.

"Well, young lady, you'll be the first to attempt the walk," Clotilde said to Laura. "I'll put a book on your head and you'll have to walk around the room without dropping it," then Clotilde took the heaviest book in the room, placed it on Laura's head so roughly it appeared she wanted to hit her with it, while the other students observed and waited for the moment Laura would drop the book.

Ms. Clotilde as well the other students didn't know that Laura growing up in her village, she not only helped her family in cleaning the humble house, but she would also accompany her father to harvest the fruits and vegetables with great care. Sometimes the crops were so good that they had enough fruits to share with everyone in the village, which filled Benjamin with joy.

They had to quickly pick up the vegetables and fruits to prevent the birds and the rabbits from damaging them and so they would carry the fruits in a basket on their head and the rest in bags within their hands. At first the basket was difficult for Laura to balance, but over time she became an expert. Once again, Laura had passed the test without difficulty, which did not please Clotilde at all.

The three magic keys

The next test focused on sitting correctly. All the students had to sit right on the edge of the chairs and then cross their legs keeping the knees together and tilting them to one side, their torso had to be straight as well and head up. The petulant Berarminia lost her balance and fell from her chair. The scholars laughed wich angered Clotilde. Although it was not an easy test for Laura, who was used to sitting on the floor or lying down on the grass, she was able to keep her balance. The day proceeded with tests and classes concerning good manners.

On the way to her room, Laura went to visit Molondrón at the stable. She wanted to make sure he was well, besides he was her only friend and she could tell him everything that had happened to her. Despite not being able to speak, Molondrón listened attentively and caressed her with his head. Laura would forgot her loneliness and nostalgia within such tender moments.

The next morning, Laura woke up very early with the singing of the roosters. She was ready to learn. She knew that it was up to her to be granted an audience with the King. Her classes for the day were about good table manners and how to use the utensils correctly, something Laura had never done before. At home they eat with their hands. It was said that the food tasted much better and was more nutritious that way.

Everyone knew that this statement wasn't true, but that it was made because the villagers did not have enough money to buy cutlery and tableware as fine and expensive as some other villagers of Arabella. They tried to be happy with what little they had. For them the most important thing was to be united; there was no wealth more valuable than shared the breaking of bread among family.

In the living room the table was set; it had things that Laura had never seen before. Luckily for her, Virginia was the teacher that day. She was a very intelligent and refined young woman, but at the same time very simple. She also came from a small village of Arabella, called Flamboyán its name is due to the flamboyán trees that are always blooming, with orange, red, and yellow colors which were very beautiful.

Just like all the girls at school Virginia arrived several years ago and was the only one in her class to get the royal shield. As a result, Flamboyán became one of the most prosperous villages in all of Arabella and Virginia was chosen to instruct the new young girls.

All the students proceeded to sit at the table with the help of the court gentlemen who chivalrously grabbed the chairs and humbly welcomed them to sit. Many of the girls were accustomed to these types of banquets, especially those who came from wealthy families and who had learned to properly behave at the table at a very young age. Estephania exemplified such a student; she was the daughter of Mr. Arcalaf, one of the richest fabric merchants in Arabella and who because of his fortune bought the title, Knight of Monte Verde, with the help of Jeremiah, a former advisor to the King.

The merchant always arrived with a servant who announced his entrance as if he was the king. His daughter, Estephania was also announced every time she came to the classroom as Miss Estephania, Los Milagros Arcalaf of Monte Verde. She only interacted with the ladies she deemed among her class. Her motive for attending the school was to reach Arabella's palace and ask the King to grant her father the title of Duke.

It was evident that Laura was very nervous and afraid. She had never eaten on a table filled with so many plates, glasses and forks with four teeth, others three and the smallest with merely two. There were also several knives; some sharp while others considerably blunt. The table was set for the likes of an army and not for ten students that represent the villages of Arabella.

Laura watched as the attendants poured the water into the fancy glasses, placed the bread in small plates on the left and observed in a bowl filled with something green and liquid, which did not look at all appetizing.

The ladies took a white cloth located to the left of the forks; some of them placed it on their neck while others on their legs as Clotilde and Virginia took notes. The outcome of these classes would determine who would best be suite to meet the demands of the royal banquet. An event in which all the kings, queens, princesses, dukes, countesses, nobles of Arabella and neighboring courts would attend. Everything had to be perfect.

Laura had not idea of what to do. She did not know where to place the cloth or napkin, as it was called by the others. Furthermore, she didn't know which utensil she should use to eat the green stuff, because she always ate with her hands and if the food was liquid she drank it with a pot made of higüero. Time passed and she had not tasted anything. This caused her to reflect on Arkazu's keys. She had already used the first one and thanks to it she was accepted into the school.

There were only two keys left and she had to use them with intelligence. But which of the two keys would be correct at that precise moment? Laura decided to use the key of *"Trust"*.

Laura remembered Arkazu's words: "The key of '*Trust"* is very powerful. It clears your doubts and gives you the courage to face any situation. It helps to believe that everything is possible, that you can achieve everything you intend if you trust yourself and your instinct." He also warned her that if she did not use it with intelligence it could be very dangerous, since you never knew what was in the minds and hearts of other people. You had to be very careful who you trusted.

Laura took a risk in applying the key of *"Trust",* particularly because she wasn't liked by the other girls and she could easily fall into a trap, believing that they were using their utensils in the right way. It could be a plan that they arranged so that she might commit a serious mistake. She was the only one who was at risk of being left out and unable to reach her goal, the others had their place insured because their families paid for them.

The key of *"Trust"* indicated that Laura must first trust herself and also had to use her instinct to avoid mistakes, advice that she once learned from her grandfather. Laura decided to observe the girls who she felt had extensive experience on the subject of etiquette that was suitable at the table.

She studied Estephania and then at Berarminia. She also saw how Laila from the village of Champiñón behaved, she was the most shyest of all, but very intelligent. Her parents forced her to go the school against her will. She had fallen in love with a man of humble means who they did not accept. They thought that if Laila could get to the palace, perhaps a noble knight would conquer her heart and she would forget about the poor mushroom grower forever. Laura also observed Abigail, but fortunately she did not follow her example, because Abigail was very gluttonous. She ate so much and so fast that she almost choked on her food.

After examining the habits of each of student, she followed the examples of those who seemed to be most confident in their table manner. She placed the napkin in her lap, delicately took a spoon and imitated the same movements as the others, inside out. The soup was a bit cold because of the time she had spent hesitating to eat and she didn't risk burning her mouth like Karmine. Although the taste of asparagus soup was not pleasant, Laura controlled her facial expressions very well.

When she saw that one of the girls stopped eating or took the napkin to clean her lips, she did the same, thus she passed the first course. Next came an entrée with contents shape like the cashew seeds that Laura loved so much, but their color was pale pink, their texture was rubbery and they were served in a glass. The servants called them fruits of the sea. She had never eaten anything like that, she couldn't even imagine what kind of fruits existed in the sea, and Laura only knew about the fruits that grew in the fields.

She wondered how the fruits grew in the sea, how the seeds could stay surrounded by so much water? In the field when it rained many of the newly planted seeds would come out of the ground and had to be replanted. She had never seen the sea, but she remembered her grandfather's stories about his journeys and the many times he accompanied the King on trips to distant lands.

Despite her inexperience, Laura continued with her plan to observe the other girls and do the same as they did. She took the small fork that had two teeth and inserted it into the fruit of the sea then placed it in her mouth. She thought that they didn't taste at all like the fruits on the land but they were not so bad.

The three magic keys

Laura continued on with the test. The main course was served and required the use the fork and knife at the same time. It was getting more complicated and exceedingly challenging for her. She thought about her parents and the villagers, she couldn't let them down, she had gone so far that giving up was not an option. With difficulty, she took the knife in her right hand and the fork on her left hand just like the others.

Clotilde was very surprised to see Laura appeared remarkably calm. Until that point everything had been fine. The cutlery had to be placed in a way that indicated that she was finished her meal and Laura was unaware. Virginia who was very kind and knew that the future of Laura and her village depended on the outcome of the test approached her, secretly letting her see a drawing that she had made illustrating the right way to leave the cutlery, without the other students and of course Clotilde noticing.

Laura looked quickly and carefully to avoid attracting the attention of Clotilde who was very attentive to everything she did. The young girl realized she had correctly placed the fork and knife wich mean she had passed the test with excellent grades, something the others could not believe thanks to Virginia's generosity, Arkazu's advice and her intelligence.

Laura was very happy. She only had to pass one more test to attend the royal banquet and have the opportunity to speak with King about the village's needs. At the end of the class she ran to see Molondrón at the stable to tell him how well she had done that day and all the new things she learned. She also told him about the fruits of sea.

After talking with her friend, Molondrón, she went to sleep and she felt ready to face the challenges at the Oratory class the next day. It was very important that all the ladies expressed themselves correctly and Laura was no exception. Although she had a beautiful voice, she needed to improve upon her us of language, learn to communicate more clearly and concisely and confidently choose words that were most suitable when addressing the King. That night Laura slept soundly, dreaming of everything she had achieved and that she going to achieve.

The next morning she was the first to arrive at the classroom. The girl was very excited because the last test had arrived. Laura was confident that she would pass the lesson. Rania Primadona from Los Lírios, a distinguished lady and socialite who married the Baron Maximiliano from the village of Los Lírios, had been chosen to teach the subject.

Rania as well as all other members of nobility had to attend and coordinate charity events. Besides being the Oratory teacher she was also in charge of organizing the royal banquet and making sure that everything went perfectly.

Rania began by placing all the girls in line and observing them one by one. The first was Catalina from the village of Carambolas followed by Karmine of Solgiral, Felicidad of Uveral, Berarminia of Pan de Frutas, Laila of Champiñon, Estephania of Monte Verde, Zoe of Flamboyán, Abigail of Damasco, Esmeralda of Los Lírios and finally Laura of Calabazas.

Rania was shocked when she saw Laura. She had never seen a girl with that feature, with ears and eyes so big and with weird spots on her cheeks in the shape of hearts; she was a strange creature. Laura felt very sad when she detected the expression on Rania's face. She immediately remembered that she was considered different from the other girls, though she still could not understand why.

The reaction she had received from Rania filled her with doubts, but above all curiosity. She wanted to know what it was about her that surprised everyone. The humble girl from Calabazas decided to uncover the mystery that surrounded her appearance after the class was over.

After the teacher's amazement, they started with the classes. Rania at first taught them how to breathe to feel calmer and control their nerves; if they do it they would be able to express their ideas clearly and without fear. Then she handed a pencil to each one of them which they had to bite it with the front teeth and recite a poem aloud. With this technique their words would come out more fluently, special for those people that have speak difficulty like Zoe who avoided talking because her stuttering.

As part of the class, each student had to demonstrate their artistic abilities like recited poetry, acted and sing. Laura chose to sing, it was something that she liked and that everyone admired in her. When she began to sing the whole room was silent. They were mesmerized by her sweet and melodious voice. It was inexplicable beauty arising from such a stranger being.

They all stood up to applaud her at the end of the song, including Clotilde and Berarminia, who although they were not very happy, they could not help but feel touched by the poor villager's voice. The class was very interesting and made Laura regain the confidence that made her forget about the mystery of her appearance. Rania asked each of them to write their speech and practice it so that when they were in front of king Amadeus they will not forget what they had to say.

Laura was ready and she continued putting into practice everything that she had learned throughout the days preceding the royal banquet. Every day she got up early and after organizing and cleaning her room she would lie on the grass and think about everything her village needed. She also remembered the kindness of her people who had placed all their trust in her.

In the village of Calabazas, Benjamin and Azucena wondered how their little girl was, if she missed them and if she had already seen her face. They were very worried about her, because they didn't know if she had accepted into the school or if she had been rejected because of her strange features, where she was, why she hadn't returned home?

Laura's parents felt guilty about the fate she had to face. She wasn't prepared to know the truth. Throughout all her life, they hid her appearance from her and made her believe that she looked the same as everybody else in the village.

Every day, Benjamin climbed to the top of the mountain and stared at the horizon. He thought that at any moment he would see the reflection of his beloved daughter.

The villagers of Calabazas were no longer the same as well. Laura had given them so much. She was very precious to them. They missed her pranks, laughter and her singing as well the hugs and kisses they received every morning from her. The grumpy shoemaker, Rigoberto, couldn't hide his sadness, tears fell from his eyes as he fixed shoes, he quickly wiped them away so that nobody would notice that his reaction to Laura's absence. He said it was the smell of the glue he used that made him cry.

Mrs. Olivia was the oldest of all the villagers in Calabazas. She had assisted in Laura's birth. She always made a cup of tea for herself and another cup of tea for her "litter girl", as she called Laura. She'd sit in her old rocking chair and talk with Laura every afternoon, who also was very talkative. The villagers of Calabazas didn't care about the royal shield or the favors of the King; they just wanted Laura to be the same happy girl as always been.

Her grandfather Enrique suffered the most after Laura's departure. He missed her so much that he had stopped eating. He no longer went to sunbathe and neglected his rose bushes, which little by little were drying up in the weeds; he didn't want to talk to anybody either.

Everyone feared that he would not bear the absence of his granddaughter and that it would lead to his dying of sadness. Calabazas was no longer the same as it had been. There was no one who didn't feel the loss of Laura's presence.

Laura however had made some friends at school; Zoe, the stutterer, Abigail who spent all her time eating, Laila who only wanted to return to the village of Champiñon and meet again with her beloved and Felicidad, who suited her name very well since she was always in a good mood. The other girls rarely spoke to her and when they did it was to make fun of her features and clothes.

She had won over Rania and Virginia, who had helped her improved her speech and manner, and she also clarified her previous confusion about the fruits of the sea. She learned that what they had served during lunch was called shrimp which were little animals that live in the sea like fish and other species.

Laura had also been taught about history and mathematics. Every day they went outside to inhale pure air. Laura took advantage of that time to explore and comprehended everything that Mother Nature gives them.

Rania and Virginia were very happy for be able to help Laura, who delighted them with her sweet voice. They knew that the task that awaited her was not easy and by her appearance she could be bullied by all the guests at the royal banquet; they are very vain people who only cared about the outside and material wealth of others, and that could be devastating for Laura.

In the meantime, Ms. Clotilde continued to conspire against the poor villager of Calabazas. She was determined to prevent at all costs that Laura reach the royal palace. Clotilde met in secret with Berarminia, Estephania, and Karmine, who were the richest and most arrogant of all. Catalina and Esmeralda were quite clumsy and could ruin everything. Therefore they didn't include them in their plan.

Berarminia wondered how it was possible for Laura not to be embarrassed about her face. If she were Laura she would not leave her room, Berarminia said. On the other hand, Estephania proposed to ruin Laura's dress for the royal banquet. However, Clotilde objected. She knew that plan wouldn't work out since Rania and Virginia will give Laura another dress to wear. Then Berarminia said, "if we put something in her tea to prevent her from talking or let alone sing?"

"That would be a good idea!" Estephania said, but Clotilde didn't agree. Then Karmine said: "We could become her best friends." "What did you just say?" The others shouted in unison, "be friends of that strange and poor creature?" Never!

Upon reflection, Clotilde stated, "that could be a good idea". The closer you are to her, the easier it will be to destroy her. Being her friend could plant the seed of insecurity in her heart and when it germinates, Laura will return to the insignificant village from which she came!

"Being like that, we accept!" Replicated Berarminia and Estephania. Thus began their plan, little by little they were approached the innocent and kind young girl of Calabazas. Although Abigail, Felicidad, Laila, and Zoe warned Laura about not to trust the others, she thought everybody deserve an opportunity, Karmine, Berarminia, and Estephania were no exception. Laura was sure that when they knew her more deeply they would end up loving her.

Laura forgot the words of Arkazú when he warned her about the key of *"Trust"*. That key could be very treacherous, for that reason she must see the inside of people before trusting them and opening her heart to them, because once inside they could hurt her a lot until the point of destroying her self-esteem...

The date of the great royal banquet was approaching and each day Berarminia, Karmine, and Estephania got closer to Laura. They gathered all her attention and left no space for the others. They praised her beautiful voice and were very kind to her. Before the three wicked girls went to sleep, they met with Ms. Clotilde to tell her all the details about their encounters with Laura during the day. They were waited for the right moment to finally attack Laura.

Laura, on the other hand, was very happy; she thought she had real friends. Every afternoon, she told Molondrón how wonderful and fun they were; very different from the ones she met when she arrived at school. Laura was confident that they truly appreciated her.

At nightfall, Laura felt nostalgic at the thought of her grandfather; she imagined the long conversations that they will have upon her return. But now it would be her who will have a new story to tell. She was very proud of everything she had learned and wanted to share with the children in her village. She made plans to teach them etiquette classes and also she thought of asking Rafael to make some cutlery for them...

The day before of the royal banquet, the teachers met with their students to finalize the details of their speeches. They rehearsed for hours, walking, sitting down, and their review the manners at the table. Everything had to be perfect; one mistake could cost them all dearly. King Amadeus was very strict and demanding with his guests, especially those who were going to ask for favors.

It is said that once, one uninvited villager dared to attend the palace and ruined the royal banquet. She had the audacity to demand the return of the taxes that her family had paid. She accuses the King of being a thief without a heart. The young woman said that her father had worked all his life to save that money and the King wasted it in fine fabrics, jewels, perfumes, and huge banquets, without caring about the suffering of his villagers.

King Amadeus, irritated by the young woman's insults, called his guards, among them the dreaded Helios who arrested the young woman for insolence and condemned her to forced labor. Her family was banished from Arabella.

The imprisoned villager, was released when she became an old woman. Nobody knows what happened to her. Some people said that she lived on the outskirts of Pan de Frutas; others said that the pain of never seeing her family again darkened her heart. She swore revenge on king Amadeus, who according to the gossips wakes up every night scared by the horrible nightmares that torment him, because he thinks that at any moment the old woman will return to get revenge on him.

All the girls were astonished and scared to know what could happen to them. Clotilde stood next to Estephania and Berarminia hearing the horror story of the women who once was a victim of the King. Although they stopped for a moment, they didn't waste time and immediately began to implement their plan which would lead Laura to reach the same fate as the unknown women from years ago.

Despite the fright of what could happen to them, the girls were enthusiastic about the big day. In their rooms, each of them chose the most beautiful dress they owned, as well as the shoes, headdresses, and jewels. They wanted to look radiant. None wanted to be overshadowed by the others.

Estephania was going to wear a dress made with the finest fabrics, since her father was the richest cloth merchant of Arabella, he bought the most expensive and beautiful silks for her daughter from a very distant lands. The dress was embroidered with gold threads, she also asks her father to make a necklace of sapphires and diamonds, and of course he pleases her. His daughter had to be the most beautiful of all, since he didn't settle for the title of Knight, he wanted the King to name him Duke of Monte Verde.

In her room, Berarminia also had a very expensive dress. It was embroidered with fine crystals, pearls and had a pure gold headdress decorated with precious stones. Although her parents were not the richest of Pan de Frutas and didn't have as much money as the Monte Verde merchant; they had very good savings and didn't skimp of used it on Berarminia. They wanted her to look spectacular at the royal banquet; they were as pretentious as she was.

Karmine, who claimed to belong to one of Solgiral's most important families, "something that was not true", since her father was a sunflowers grower he had to work from sunrise to sunset to support his family, but his wife Acacia and his daughter Karmine were never satisfied with what he could provide. So, he was forced to borrow some coins for which he had to pay large interest just to please his family. Poor Stanislaus he did not dare to contradict Acacia; she did everything possible to catch a rich and powerful husband for her daughter and that way they can get out of poverty.

Acacia was sure that Karmine's beauty was enough to conquer a noble knight. That's the reason why she did not hold back on spending the coins the Stanislaus had borrowed to buy a beautiful dress and ornaments that would make her daughter stand out from the others.

Zoe, Laila, and Felicidad, also had beautiful and extravagant gowns for the royal banquet. Although Laila was not very happy because she missed her beloved of Champiñón, she was prepare for the big day only to please her father, who had the hope that a handsome and noble knight would conquer her heart and therefore she forget once and for all about the poor grower of mushrooms.

Meanwhile, Abigail had problems with her dress. The anxiety caused by the idea of appears in front of the King, had made her eat more than usual. Everyone knew that she was very greedy and that she spent all her time eating cakes, but in the last few weeks she had gained several kilos and the dress that her father buy for her from the neighboring country of Alcalante no longer fitted her.

Abigail's father believed that if his daughter looked very beautiful, she could conquer the heart of a noble gentleman and she would stop eating a least a little bit. But Abigail didn't care that her dress didn't suit her. The only thing she cared about it was the food, and she was madly in love with desserts.

While the others measured their dresses, Catalina was in her room trying to walk with her new heels. Every time she took a step she fell. Catalina had to hold on to everything she could to keep standing.

Esmeralda was not the exception; she didn't even know where to start. Every time she tried to wear the dress she put it on backward. Esmeralda ended up putting the huge chintz over her dress. She still did not learn to differentiate it from the skirt... And so they all prepared to appear in front of King Amadeus.

In her small room, Laura unwrapped all the gifts that the villagers of Calabazas give her. She already had used the perfume and the lip balm from

Maravides. She would wear the sandals that Rigoberto had made for her and were painted by Rafaelo with coral colors and had small stones as well as flowers and butterflies made by his young students.

Rigoberto thought that Laura was a caterpillar and one day she would become a beautiful butterfly. Mrs. Gervasia cultivated the most beautiful flowers of all Arabella and she made for Laura a beautiful crown to adorn her head.

The crown was made with a mix of flowers and each of them had a very special meaning: violet to keep hope, gardenia for joy, geranium in memory of their friendship, begonia for her kindness, clementine as the beauty of her soul, flower plum tree to be strong and keep her promise, laurel for her nobility, and flowers of honeysuckle and magnolias as a symbol of love bonds that bind Laura to her family and everyone in the village.

Enrique gave Laura a pearl that he had found on the shores of the Sea of Su in one of his many trips. He remembered that he jealously hid the pearl from the King's guards. It was his gift to his beloved Rita, his wife and lifelong companion, whom he hadn't seen for a long time because of traveling. Enrique was eager to return to Calabazas to give such a valuable jewel to someone who had given him everything.

Upon returning from what was his last trip, Enrique asked the King to allow him to stay in Arabella that way he could be closer to his wife who was very ill. He asked the King to instead be accompanied by another of his servants on his trips to other kingdoms. The king understood and accepted he request.

When Enrique returned to Calabazas with the precious pearl, he found an empty chair and his little daughter Azucena in dismay. His great love had died the same day he departure to the sea. He could not believe it. What he most regretted was that neither the biggest pearl nor the most expensive stones could replace the treasure he had lost.

Enrique kept the pearl in a small box which he only reopened the day Laura departure to the big city. He made a small hole on the pearl and passed a thin thread through, then he tied the ends for her be able to use it as a necklace.

Laura was opening each of her gifts until she finally opened a large package. This was delicately wrapped with large and broad leaves from the forest. When she removed the last leaves, her eyes sparkled, it was the most beautiful dress she had ever seen, worthy of a princess.

The dress was made by Carmelia, who took advantage of the hours that Laura used to take the tea with Mrs. Olivia, to sew it. Carmelia wanted to surprise Laura with the dress, and yes she did it! All the villagers brought the finest pieces of cloth they had, it was all they could give. They didn't have enough coins to buy an expensive gown, and much less embroidered in gold or silver as the other young girl.

Carmelia joined each piece and little by little, it was given a shape. It was beautiful! The dress was a mixture of textures and bright colors; it looked like a rainbow in its entire splendor. All the love and kindness of the villagers of Calabazas was reflected on the dress. Laura did not doubt that this would be the best day of her life. She couldn't wait for it to arrive and spent the night counting the hours to see the new and wonderful sunrise.

The teacher Ms. Clotilde, Karmine, Berarminia, and Estephania, could not wait for the day to come neither. They had everything ready, the next morning they would take Laura for a walk in the school gardens, but not where they used to walk, this time they would go near the lake.

In their conversations with Laura they discovered that Laura had never seen her face, and she did not know what a mirror was. In her village nobody had ever mentioned it.

When Estephania asked her if she used to fetch for water in the river, Laura replied that she was never allowed to go near the river since her parents thought it was very dangerous for her. They preferred that she stayed in the village helped their neighbors. With his information Clotilde concluded that the reason why Laura was not ashamed of herself, despite the ridiculously insults and rejections she had received was because she doesn't know how she looks. So it was obvious that the only way to destroy her was to show her who she really was. Someone very different from the others.

Esmeralda unable to find a way to put on her dress went to ask Catalina for help. When suddenly she heard a murmur coming from Estephania's room. Esmeralda approached stealthily and without being noticed listened at the precise moment when the wicked gathered conspiring against Laura.

Although Esmeralda was not Laura's friend, she didn't dislike her presence either. She thought of warning Laura the next morning. Esmeralda was afraid to go out and look for Laura in the middle of the night. She decided to way until they see each other in the morning.

Very early in the morning, Abigail ran to Laura room to ask for help. Like all the girls in Calabazas Laura helped the seamstress to stick buttons, to make eyelets and hemlines; so who better than her to help Abigail with her dress. Laura, as always so kind went to help Abigail. She brought with her a cloth in which she kept some threads and needles that she used to mend her clothes, they were so old that when she washed them one or other side ripped off and she had to sew them again.

Zoe, Laila, and Felicidad were all in Abigail's room helping her get into that dress which was so tight that it didn't close. It was an impossible mission, Zoe replied: " I tol-tol-told you not- not-not to –to-to eat so-so-so much cak-cak-cake ". But now it was too late for sermons; they had to find a solution.

Laura had the brilliant idea to replace the buttons of the dress and instead make eyelets, then cut a piece of cloth from the ring and sew a long thin ribbon with it, proceeded to pass the placement through the eyelets from one side to another, as if she had knitted her hair.

Rita Mendoza

She asked Abigail to put on her dress once more, pulling the ends of the ribbon and made a nice bow at the end, finally she fixed the dress roll; they were surprised, the dress fit perfectly.

Abigail for her part was very grateful to Laura. "I had nothing to worry about!" exclaimed Abigail, to whom Felicidad replied: "that is very true!" With the new dress adjustments, you will be able to eat everything you wanted. Something you couldn't do with the buttons that your dress had because it was very possible that they could explode in the middle of the banquet and one of them fell into the King's soup". They all laughed with the occurrences of Felicidad.

When Laura was about to return to her room since there were only a few hours left for the big royal banquet and like other girls she had to get ready, Berarminia, Estephania, and Karmine appeared. All of them showing their best smile when they saw Laura, they invited her to take a walk through the garden, Laura was not sure about going, she had to be ready at the time indicated by the teachers because they all would leave together to the royal palace.

After the insistence of her "friends", she agreed to accompany them only for a few minutes. While they were walking through the garden, they question Laura about her family, her village and everything she would ask the King that day. The naive girl from Calabazas did not realize how far she was from the school.

When they reached the forest, they decided to sit near a crystal clear water lake, so transparent that it looked like a mirror, under the pretext that the water of that lake was magical and if they washed their faces with it they would look even more beautiful than they were. The first to wash her face was Karmine and then Estephania, both said how wonderful they felt and that their skin was softer and smoother.

Berarminia motivated Laura to go wash her faces at the lake because that day she had to look very beautiful too. Laura innocently agreed and went to the lake; she was a bit afraid because she had never been close to one, not even the river in her village.

The three evil girls were anxiously waiting for the moment when Laura saw her reflection in the water for the first time in her life. She approached slowly to the shore of the lake and while she sticking her head in the water, she saw something terrible. She did not know what it was, but that it had long ears, huge eyes, and spots on her cheeks, it was something strange that she saw. She was frightened so much that she thought it was some monster in the lake, when she tried to retreated she fell sitting down.

The others began to laugh and Laura did not understand why. Then Berarminia said to Laura: "Are you frightened of your face? Do you think that we are not afraid to see you too? Estephania and Karmine shouted that she was a monster, that she should be locked up so she would not scare people away, because no one in the world had ears and eyes as big as hers and much less those heart-shaped spots on her cheeks. Now, Laura understood why nobody wanted to be her friend.

The young girl burst into tears, she could not believe that the image she saw in the lake was hers, and much less those to whom she gave her friendship were so cruel and evil. Berarminia, Estephania, and Karmine went back to school to get ready for the big royal banquet. They were laughing all the way, they were happy!

At the school, Clotilde impatiently waited for the return of the young girls, she walked from one place to another, thinking about their goal. When she heard them arrive, she immediately went to the garden so that Ms. Rania and Mss. Virginia would not notice Laura's absence and look around for her.

The harpies were so euphoric that Clotilde could not understand what they were saying until she ordered them to be silent. Once calm, they began to tell her everything that had happened and the fact that Laura made when she saw herself for the first time. They had not doubt that they finished with Laura and that she wouldn't show up at the banquet. Clotilde happily thought that Laura had hopefully disappeared forever in the forest, because a being like that should be in a cave. So she ordered to the girls not to say anything about what happened…

Meanwhile in the village of Calabazas, Laura's mother felt a very strong pain in her chest. She felt that her heart wanted to get out of grief; she didn't understand the reason and she hide from Benjamin her sadness. She knew something was happening to her beloved daughter. The sky of Calabazas was covered with black clouds, something unusual at that time of the year. All the villagers sensed that something bad was about to happen and asked God to take care of Laura.

In the forest, sobbing and devastated was Laura. She felt that her heart had broken into a thousand pieces. She could not believe that all her life had been deceived by the people she loved most.

She thought that everyone in the village felt sorry for her and not love and that's why they hid the truth about her feature. She did not understand how they had told her that she look the same to all of them and moreover that she was beautiful, when in fact it was not so.

Laura was alone, disappointed of everyone even in herself. Her self-esteem had vanished and she stopped believing. She lost her confidence and hope. Now she was ashamed of whom she was. She opened her heart to people who only wanted to hurt her. Only then she understood Arkazu's advice when he told her about the power of the key of ***"Trust"*** and how treacherous it could be. Everything was lost for her; the village of Calabazas would never be the same again!

In the meantime, at the main hall of the school, Rania, Virginia, and Clotilde waited for the girls to finish getting ready. It was almost time to go to the royal palace and everything seemed to be in order. One by one they entered the room, they looked beautiful with their long and baggy dresses made with the most delicate and fine fabrics and embroidered in threads of gold and silver. Some were covered with sparkling crystals and pearls.

Their elaborate hairstyles were adorned with gold headdresses with encrusted gemstones, as well as the necklaces they wore. All were worthy of admiration!

It was time to leave, but Mss. Virginia noticed that among all of them, they were missing someone very special, nothing more and nothing less than the sweet and kind young girl of Calabazas, Laura. It was very strange that she had not yet reached the room, she was always very punctual. Rania asked the other girls if they had seen her, to which Abigail, Zoe, Laila, and Felicidad, responded that she was with them very early that morning helping Abigail with her dress and after that they didn't see her again.

Berarminia, Estephania, and Karmine denied having seen her that day. They explained that they had spent the whole morning with Ms. Clotilde finalizing some details of their presentation and of course the Clotilde confirmed their statement since she was also part of the macabre plan that she not going to ruin.

Meanwhile, Virginia went to look for Laura in her room. Virginia thought that maybe she had some mishap with her dress and maybe she could help.

Esmeralda, who was so confused, forgot what she had heard the night before in Estefania's room. She was so focused on not making a fool of herself at the banquet that she thought of nothing else but that. Catalina, for her part, still did not dominate the heels on her feet; whenever she tried to take a step her feet were bent sideways and she had to hold on to Esmeralda to avoid falling.

When Virginia arrived at Laura's room, she knocked on the door, without an answer. She walked inside and she saw the dress that Laura would wear that day on her bed, next to it was a wreath of flowers and a thread with a beautiful pearl. Her sandals were on the floor, but Laura was nowhere to be found. Mss. Virginia went to look for her at the stable where her friend Molondrón was, she always went there to talk to him, but she was not there either.

Virginia was very worried; she did not know where Laura was and much less would suspect what happened to her. Since the previous day everything was really good, Laura was very happy to attend the royal banquet, so she did not understand what happened or where she had gone. The time passed quickly and it was getting late, Rania and Laura's friends were visibly distressed, they could not believe that Laura would not come to the banquet since it was the opportunity that she and her village were waiting for many years. All the villagers had put their hopes in her, the gifts they gave her were not the most expensive or fine, but they were made with so much love.

Back in the schoolroom, Clotilde insisted that they had to leave without Laura! "It is clear that this young lady did not care that we had lost our time, and she couldn't snub the King" replied the evil teacher. When Virginia entered the room she had no choice but to tell them that Laura had left.

Zoe, Abigail, Laila, and Felicidad could not believe what they were hearing, the joy they had in their faces turned into sadness, and they learned to love her as she was. On the other hand, Karmine could not hide her happiness, she looked at her accomplices Berarminia and Estephania making a gesture that the plan had worked. Clotilde immediately requested to the servants to bring the carriage that would take them to the royal palace.

As they walked away from the school, Rania, Virginia and Laura's friends searched incessantly with their eyes through the windows of the carriage for some sign of her. They lost hope when they saw nothing that trailed Laura's path.

The three magic keys

Laura was still crying with sadness, she was devastated feeling that her life did not make sense. Suddenly, she heard footsteps approaching among the dry leaves of the forest. When she raising her head, in front of her was the old man Arkazú. He looked at her with kind eyes and sat down beside her in silence.

They lasted a while without saying a word. Laura thought that he was disappointed with her because she placed her trust in those who didn't deserve it. Arkazú, who was very wise, could read what happened in her face. He could see the sadness in her heart. He also realized that she had lost love and self-confidence, she had stopped believing.

_" I know it's very painful to be betrayed by the people in whom you placed your trust; I also know that it hurt you to discover your exterior, because you always assumed that you were like the other people in your village. I know that caused you a big wound in your heart", Arkazú said.

_ "Life is like a blank canvas _ Arkazú continued_ each of us has the power to paint it with the colors we want. In that canvas we can express our emotions, feelings and desires, as well as our frustrations and failures. It is for this reason that some people choose to paint their canvas with dark colors as a reflection of their shortcomings, ambition, selfishness, evilness and envy that they carry in their hearts and as a result of this they obscure the lives of others...

On the other hand, others choose to paint it with light, cheerful and vibrant colors, full of life, kindness, hope, compassion and love, so that everyone who sees it can feel happy and grateful. Although others try to splash their canvases by planting weeds, hatred and resentment, they will never be able to obscure them because they have a positive attitude towards life and this is more powerful than the wickedness of those people.

Arkazú also told her about Pandora: "Each person decides their destiny. The young woman who demanded the King to return the money that her family had managed to collect with so much sacrifice and work was not an evil person, on the contrary. Pandora's heart was noble and pure, she suffered when she saw her old and sick father go out every morning to cultivate the land so he could be able to bring food to the house, meanwhile in the royal palace they wasted everything they took away from the poor villagers in banquets, precious and expensive jewels all of that without caring about the suffering of their people, they were indifferent to their poverty.

Pandora was filled with anger against the King Amadeus and was condemned to spend her life as a slave until she became an old woman. The pain she felt was so deep that she allowed the darkness to cover her heart. Pandora became a wicked being, full of hatred and rancor, she swore revenge on the King, but the person who paid the consequences of his punishment was your mother.

_ My mother? _ Laura ask surprised.

_ That's right, your mother was her victim. Arkazú replied.

_ When the beautiful and young Azucena went to the big city, trying to get the royal shield for her village, like you, she was deceived by Pandora, who with a sigh stole her brightness and the freshness of her youth and she cast a curse on her. Laura could not believe what the knowledgeable Arkazú was telling her about her mother, never had anyone in the village told her about what had happened, not even her own mother.

Laura thought she was the first young girl in Calabazas to go to the big city, because the villagers did not have enough coins to afford the trip and the reason why they sent her at this time was because they really needed the intervention of the King. The village had grown so much in recent years that food was scarce and not enough for everyone, help was needed urgently.

Arkazú continued: _ I was near the stream when I saw your mother, she was weak and disoriented, then I knew what Pandora had done to her. I warned her that if she did not return as soon as possible to Calabazas, Pandora's curse would fall on the whole village...

Your mother had the option to continue on her way to the big city and allow Pandora's curse to cover all Calabazas, so she would not be the only victim of the vile old woman. However, she decided to return to the village, it was more important for her to save the lives of the villagers than her own. She was willing to sacrifice herself for everyone".

Azucena could also choose to be cruel and evil like Pandora since both were noble and innocent young woman, but she searched inside her heart and opened the doors of "Gratitude". Just like you, your mother also had that key. By opening the doors of "Gratitude" she was able to search among her most precious memories, love, and kindness. Azucena was grateful for all the affection she had received from everyone around her, she also appreciated every day lived, every breath.

She was thankful for nature, for the animals, for the breeze that brushed her hair, she was grateful for all that was good, but she also felt appreciation for the difficult times and situations she had to go through, because she knew that behind the darkness there is always a ray of light. Azucena also knew that life was made up of lessons needed to learn and that despite the difficult test, something positive would be found in it...

When you are pure and grateful, the bad things that happen to you, as well as what happened to your mother are insignificant, because love is so strong that it doesn't allow darkness to cover the heart and for that reason, the curse of Pandora did not consummated on her.

Arkazú carried on, didn't your parents, your grandpa and all of the villagers given you love? Do you think they do it out of compassion? They do it because they truly love you and are grateful to God for having you. They do not see how different you are, they only see the nobility that is inside you, it is what matters, and it is what makes you beautiful. Laura interrupted Arkazú and asked him: _ how could I be grateful for the bad things that had happened to me? How I can feel

Rita Mendoza

gratitude when I'm a victim of evil? What was the positive thing I will find in them?

_ Look at the sky_ Arkazú said to her and search inside you. There you will find the answer". Laura looked at the sky trying to find the answers to her questions.

The royal palace was ready to welcome all the guests and begin the largest and most awaited banquet of all Arabella and neighboring kingdoms. Up there came kings with their wives, beautiful princesses, who wore their tiaras and majestic dresses chosen for the occasion, the princes, dukes, and counts, wore their uniforms with the highest insignia of their kingdoms, the nobles and the most illustrious knights from neighboring districts were also present.

For the banquet, the most outstanding musicians of all Arabella were hired, as well as recognized chefs and confectioners, who prepared exquisite delicacies for the delight of all the guests. At the request of king Amadeus, the best wine of the West was served. The living room was decorated with the most beautiful flowers from each of the villages.

The tables were dressed with fine tablecloths matched all the cutlery, glassware and dinnerware with the royal shield engraved on them. Everything was exaggeratedly wonderful.

The carriage with the teachers and the nine young ladies of the school made their entrance to the palace. The huge doors of the palace were opened for them. They were all open-mouthed; they could not believe everything their eyes saw. Karmine imagined herself living there, it was just what she deserved, and at least that's what she thought.

Berarminia was so restless to enter the royal room where the banquet was held that she fell from the carriage tearing her dress. The other girls could not contain themselves and burst out laughing, including Estephania and Karmine who were her accomplices, but at the same time, they were also her rivals. Each one of them only cared to capture the attention of the guests, especially the King so that he would grant their requests.

Abigail, ironically told Berarminia: "It's a shame that Laura is not here with us, because she is the only one who could help you with your dress". Berarminia with an angry face had to reach the living room with her torn dress and that didn't allow her to enjoy the royal banquet.

Karmine, for her part, did not waste the time to get close to all the handsome gentlemen she saw alone. Her goal and also that of her mother too, was that she would conquer a young nobleman and if one of them were the heirs to Arabella's crown, much better. To her bad luck, many of the gentlemen she approached were already engaged and others preferred to talk with someone more intelligent and interesting than her, so they ignored her completely.

Estephania, on the other hand, was looking for a way to get to the King to ask for what her father had entrusted to her. Unlike the other gentlemen who were present at the banquet, Estephania's father, Jeremiah had not been invited, as he was not of high rank, and everyone knew that he had bought the title of Knight of Monte Verde. The greedy Jeremiah had been one of the councilors of the palace for a long time and took advantage of his position to convince the King to grant him that title.

The King's sentinel, the dreaded and muscular Helios, did not let Estephania get close to the throne where King Amadeus was sitting, along with other kings and queens who were his most distinguished guests that day, so she unsuccessfully tried to sneak in various ways.

Abigail did not leave the dessert tables, everything was delicious and she wanted to try each one of them. For her fortune she did not have to worry about her dress; the arrangement that Laura had made was perfect when she felt that it was too tight she could just loosening the tapes a little to have more space in the stomach piece to continue filling it with sweets.

Zoe found an admirer who had a lot, but a lot of patience as she took a long time to say a phrase, her difficulty speaking and the nerves that the handsome man produced her, made her stutter more and more, as you can imagine.

Laila was sad and kept thinking about her lover, she was so eager to return to Champiñón that when some handsome young man tried to come to talk with her, she would change places with Felicidad; she felt that her heart already had an owner, besides she did not have anything to fear at that moment, she was luckily that her father was not present to see how she ignored the suitors.

Felicidad was the life of the party! She would laugh, and make jokes. She enjoyed watching people dance, she forgot everything that she had learned in the etiquette classes, especially what Ms. Clotilde had told her, "educated and high-born people should only smile rather than laugh", much less laugh as Felicidad did.

Catalina did not let go of Esmeralda for a moment, she was afraid of falling in her heels and even though she had practiced walking with them, it was impossible to achieve it, she was used to wearing sandals and running barefoot in the woods.

After the banquet passed, Ms.Clotilde annoyed by the laughter of Felicidad, whom she constantly scolded, but she did not pay attention to her and Mss.Virginia and Ms. Rania were still worried about Laura.

In the forest looking up to the sky, trying to find out what was the lesson she had to learn and the reasons why she should feel grateful, there was the unfortunate young girl of Calabazas, who without realizing was left alone, the wise Arkazú had disappeared silently... Suddenly a light breeze blew her face and in that instant, she knew what she had to do.

She ran back to her small room, where she cleaned herself up, sprinkled some of the perfume that Maravides had given her and put on the shiny dress that Carmelia had made for her, as well the sandals that Rigoberto and

Rafaelo had worked so hard. She put on the necklace with the pearl that her grandfather gave her and adorned her hair with the crown of flowers that Gervasia wove. She couldn't forget to take the three keys that Arkazú gave her. She ran to the stable in search of her cart and Molondrón. In a rush they went to the royal palace, Laura was determined to face her destiny.

In the palace, King Amadeus sat on his throne ready to listen the requests of his people, especially those of the young girls who represented the nine villages of Arabella.

The first one to be announced was Miss Berarminia from Pan de Frutas; Clotilde had to take her off from her seat because she didn't want to stand up due her torn dress. At last, Clotilde made Berarminia walked, she felt the looks of the guests on her; she could hear the murmurs and laughter discreetly, she felt so ashamed that when she was in front of the King, she only managed to bow and immediately ran away; at that moment no one could contain the laughter.

Then, it was Miss Karmine of Solgiral's turn, who thought that the moment she had been waiting for had finally arrived, in which all the handsome gentlemen would contemplate her beauty catching one of them. Karmine walked towards the King with her head straight and when she was in front of him, she asked for the favor to marry one of his heirs, as it would be an honor for the fortunate one to marry the most beautiful girl of all Arabella. The King could not comprehend what he was hearing, much less his descendants who were engaged in marriage to other young ladies of a higher bloodline. Among the King's heirs was his grandson Matias who would marry the beautiful and rich Scarlet, daughter of the king of Prada and successor to the throne.

The King asked Karmine, what were her merits or those of her family to request the hand of one of his heirs. She was very arrogant like her mother Acacia; she only stated that her beauty was her greatest merit.

King Amadeus called her insolent, and said: "Do you think that outer beauty is everything in life? I would never allow one of my descendants to marry a pretentious, petulant, ambitious girl like you and your family! Do you think I do not know what intentions you and your mother have? Get out of my sight!" shouted the King in front of everyone.

Now, it was Miss Estephania of Los Milagros Arcalaf of Monte Verde's turn, the young girl asked the sentry to announce her. Estephania, seeing the King's reaction to Karmine's request, approached very quietly. When facing him, she bowed and began to praise the goodness and gifts of the King, saying:

"Oh your Majesty, my King. The most noble and beloved King of all the ends of the earth, who has received the grace of heaven to govern with wisdom. I'm Estephania the humblest of your vassals. I lean in front of your feet, to ask you generously to grant me the request that I ask of naming my father Duke of Monte Verde. He is one of the most faithful and collaborator of your servants... my father, the illustrious Knight of Monte Verde!

King Amadeus subtly replied: "Oh my sweet and humble Estephania of Monte Verde, you had honored me with your words that are more cloying than honey, with which you try to praise me, and so I grant your father a title. What a small favor you ask!"

Do you think that I am going to name your father a Duke? Your father is nothing but a greedy merchant, who has amassed his fortune by deceiving the villagers with cheap materials, which he sells at such a high price as if they were the finest fabrics of all kingdoms. Neither you nor your father deserves to hold that title or any other! From this moment I withdraw your father the title of

Knight of Monte Verde for not being worthy of it. Estephania visibly angry, left throwing tantrums.

The other girls were very nervous, especially Catalina and Esmeralda, who decided to face the King together. They were announced as Misses Catalina of Carambolas and Esmeralda of Los Lírios.

Both of them holding hands could not help shivering in front of the King. They bowed as the teachers had taught them and proceeded to make their request. Catalina asked for more land to be given to the villagers of Carambolas, considering the population had grown so much lately that they did not have enough land for the cultivation of the fruit that was their sustenance.

For her part, Esmeralda requested from the King's to build a stone path that would allow the villagers travel to others villages to sell the lily flowers that would increase their income for the benefit of all including the King himself.

After hearing the requests of Catalina and Esmeralda, the king Amadeus ordered that they be fulfilled, since he considered that, unlike the previous ones, they asked for the welfare of their villages and the King himself. The coffers of the palace would increase with the collection of taxes;

likewise King Amadeus ordered that each of them be given the royal shield as a symbol that he would fulfill his promises.

Then it was the turn of Miss Zoe of Flamboyán. She accepted that her admirer help her explain to the King what she required, because of what had happened with Karmine and Estephania, she did not want to upset the King. She thought that he would not have too much patience with her stuttering.

Through her admirer she asked the King to built a school for the children of the villagers of Flamboyán, they didn't know how to read or write because their parents did not have enough money to pay for their studies. She also told the King that if all the villagers had the opportunity to go to school, they would learn new trades and this would make Arabella the most powerful kingdom in the world. The King agreed with her request and also granted her the long-awaited royal shield.

Miss Felicidad of Uveral was also announced, and as usual, she was very happy. After curtsy, she requested from the King to taste the wine that she had brought as a gift to his Majesty. She was sure that he had never in his life drank such pleasing wine, which was developed by the grape growers of her village. She assured that it was the best of all the wines in the world.

The King agreed to taste the wine, but before he gave it to his guard Helios to taste as was his custom, so if someone had poisoned it, that someone would not be him. After Helios tasted the wine without causing any ill effects, the King also did it and it was indeed excellent, better than the expensive wines he bought from distant lands for his banquets.

Felicidad took advantage of the King's pleasure for the wine and request from him instead of giving benefits to other lands, buy the wine produced by the villagers of Uveral, so everyone would win, because their crops and income would increase and the King and his guests would be very pleased.

The King without releasing the glass of wine and without thinking twice requested that Uveral villagers send him all the barrels of wine they had and he promised to continue buying their wine. Felicidad was happier than ever for what she had accomplished and of course for the royal shield.

When they announce Miss Abigail from Damasco village, she had eaten so much that she felt that her stomach was going to explode. She lost all manners to the point of lying on the floor. Consequently, two sentinels had to help her stand up; her face was full of fruit cake.

The King could not believe that a young lady behaved in such a way, but after the wine from Uveral he was in a very good mood. Abigail asked the King to declare the Damasco's day or apricot, one of the most delicious fruits of the whole kingdom. She also explained that with this holiday her village would attract the attention of the other villages and neighboring kingdoms, which will go to taste the magnificent desserts of damascos that the villagers prepared.

"Ha, ha, ha!" The King laughed, Abigail's request seemed very funny, but who better than her to know about the delights they prepare in her village. Still, it seemed like a good idea for each village to have a holiday to promote its products and attract more people to the kingdom.

Abigail was so happy! If she ate for being nervous before, now she would eat for joy. She was sure that on her return to Damasco they would receive her with a big banquet with her favorite foods for bringing the royal shield to the village.

Finally, they called Miss Laila de Champiñón. Although it was not her desire to attend the royal banquet because she preferred to be close to her beloved, Laila very respectfully request from the King to reduce the taxes that the mushroom growers had to pay. In this way they would lower the selling price of their products and more people could buy them, not only in her village, but also in the other neighboring villages and beyond.

The King didn't understand how that could benefit him? Abigail explained that the villagers preferred to eat other vegetables rather than mushrooms, because they were very expensive, which caused the mushrooms to be damaged. For that reason the taxes paid by their growers were not so significant to the King, but if everyone in the village could pay a fair price for the mushrooms, the demand would increase and they would sell even more.

_ Oh! I understand, _ said the king _. "If I reduce the taxes, they'll lower their sales price too, and all the villagers will buy the mushrooms and therefore the growers have to cultivate more to be able to please people. That will give them more money and they will be able to pay the taxes without difficulty. It seems good a idea! I will lower the taxes on mushrooms and all the products of the villages so that way everybody can eat properly.

Laila breathed a sigh of relief, knowing that her beloved was going to be able to pay his taxes and he would also harvest more mushrooms and so her father would not see him as a poor farmer. That filled her heart with hopes; she was anxious to return with the royal shield to the village of Champiñón and give the good news...

There was no one else to be announced, therefore the King was about to leave the room. Suddenly there was a noise coming from the palace's door, everyone turned to see what it was.

They were surprised to see a young girl getting off an old cart pulled by a donkey. The girl had a beautiful and bright multicolored dress, on her head she wore a wreath of flowers and her pleasant perfume could be perceived from the distance.

The young girl stopped for a moment at the entrance of the room. She closed her eyes and opened them slowly, she looked at the three golden and shining keys that she was holding in her hands and then she continued. The girl was covered by a bright light, it seemed as if she was floating in the air. She was singing while walked down the wide hall of the room, leaving everyone shocked.

The three magic keys

What everyone present heard was simply beautiful! Everyone including the King wondered who she was. Ms. Clotilde who was near to the main entrance of the room, was surprised to see that the young girl was Laura. Immediately Ms. Rania approached the King and told him the name of the girl... Laura of Calabazas. Upon hearing the name of the village, king Amadeus was speechless. It had been a very long time since someone from Calabazas attended the royal banquet.

When Laura was in front of king Amadeus, she politely curtsy him. The King approached her, looked at her and instantly knew who she was. He held her tightly and tears began to fall. The guests did not understand what was happening, they never saw the King embrace a commoner, let alone cry.

King Amadeus asked her: "Are you the daughter of Azucena and Benjamin? Are you the granddaughter of my faithful and most beloved servant Enrique?" To which Laura responded with an affirmation.

_ "I never thought that this moment would come!" Said the King. "Before you make your request, I want to ask you to forgive me for the damage I caused to you and your family.

Many years ago when I took possession of the throne after inherited it from my father, being an inexperienced youth man, I allowed myself to be guided by arrogant and greedy people who only cared about wasting the kingdom's money on jewels, fabrics, and banquets while making the villagers pay high taxes.

_ One of the kingdom's advisors at that time was Jeremiah, the most ambitious of all. He did not satisfied with the coins he collected for himself from each villager; he hid the coins from the kingdom and also sold royal titles to people without lineage and scruples like the fabric merchant named Arcalaf from the village of Monte Verde.

_ Without realizing it in time, I let myself be enveloped by Jeremiah, who advised me to cruelly punish a young woman who came in front of me to demand the return of her family savings. _The King went on to recount what happened to the young woman, who accused him of stealing money from her family: _ "I condemned her to forced labor during her life and banished her family from Arabella".

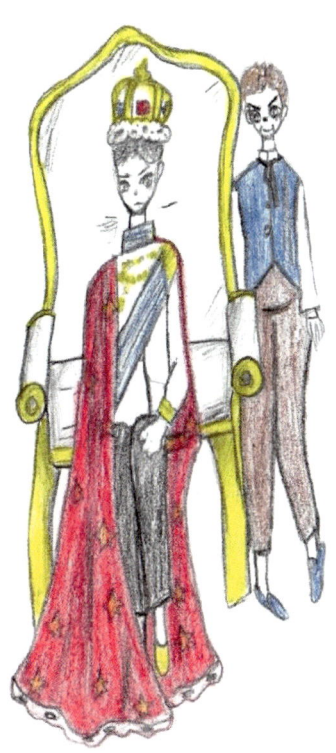

Rita Mendoza

_ I always followed the example of my father who was an honest man and could not allow his memory to get dirty, besides he had never stolen anything from anyone. I never thought that one of my closest advisers would be capable of such an atrocious act.

When king Amadeus discovered what Jeremiah had done, it was too late and although he ordered Pandora's release, she had already become an old woman. He wanted to compensate her for the damage he had caused. However, Pandora did not accept it and instead she swore to take revenge on him. The King never imagined that she would do it through the daughter of his most loyal servant, who grew up with him and became his best and only friend!

_ Since the day, when your mother Azucena was cursed by Pandora, I never saw my friend again. My guilt was so big that I didn't dare to look for him; I did not feel worthy to look him at his eye...

_ Despite of all these years I was aware of my good friend Enrique. I always asked one of my soldiers to go to the village of Calabazas and without Enrique realizing, I would find out how he was doing and what I could do to repair the damage I caused. Back in the palace, my sentinel told me everything about Enrique and his family, he told me that despite the shortcomings and difficulties he was going through, Enrique was very happy with his little granddaughter to whom he told about his journeys. The guard also told me that the little girl was very different from the other children and that he had never seen anyone like her.

_ Sometimes I thought of sending the family some gold coins so they would not have to worry, but I knew Enrique so well that if I only dared to try, he would despise me. He was always an honest, loyal and hard-working man; he would never accept a single penny that he didn't earn. So I stayed a distant. Knowing that he was happy sustained me...

_ During all these years, I tried to hide my sadness by showing myself invincible, but the pain never left me. Now that you know that the culprit of your misfortune has been me, I can understand that you do not want to forgive me, _ said the King.

The room was in deep silence just like Laura. No one could believe what happened. Berarminia who was in a corner away from everyone felt so sorry for what she had done, she understood why Laura was so different from all of them.

Laura, finally found in her heart the answer she had so much sought. She found the meaning of the key of *"Gratitude"*, she understood that every person in that room had been victims of evil in some way or another. She also believed in the existence of true love, and in the ability of forgiveness, just as her mother and grandfather did.

Her grandfather never returned to the palace, it was not because he resented the King for what Pandora had done to his daughter Azucena. It was because he decides to stay in the village to take care of them. Enrique remembered the King with great affection.

Although he was just another servant of the palace, Amadeus considered him a great friend, especially after the death of his father King Adolfo, who earned the respect and affection of the people in Arabella. He was very kind so Amadeus strove to be equal to him and continue his legacy.

When ascending to the throne, the young King requested the advice of his friend Enrique, who although was not one of the councilors of the palace, he always told the King to get closer to the villagers and listen to their requests as his father did.

The relationship between the King and Enrique caused made the counselors of the palace feel jealous of Enrique. On several occasions, they attended some traps to make him look bad in front of the king, but Amadeus knew his friend so well that he did not give credit to the accusations that rose up against Enrique.

Enrique never asked for anything for himself or his family despite his closeness to the King. He preferred to follow the rules of Arabella, in which the petitions had to be made by the representatives of each of the villages. Unfortunately, Enrique was not present the day that both Pandora and Amadeus were the unfair victims of the evil Jeremiah, who deliberately did everything possible so that the girl was condemned and could not accuse him of having stolen the money from her family.

The King, felt aggrieved by young Pandora and hearing the bad advice of Jeremiah, did so. That day King Amadeus had granted Enrique permission to leave the palace to accompany his wife Rita in the birth of his daughter Azucena, for this reason, Laura's grandfather could not stop the unjust and cruel punishment that condemned Pandora.

Despite everything that happened with his daughter, Enrique never blamed king Amadeus, although he did not justify his action, he was touched to see Pandora turned into an old woman, but he knew that only she was responsible for cultivating negative feelings that little by little were extinguishing her love and gratitude for life, she let the evil darken her heart.

Laura looked at the King in the eyes and reply that the damage was already done and that there was no way to go back in time to repair the past, but it is time to remedy the present. Laura gave him the keys she had received from the wise Arkazú. She told the King that with those keys he could open the three most important doors of life and that those doors were inside his heart. She was giving each one of them while deciphering its meaning.

First, she gave him the key of *"**Love**"*, so that he would let out all the love that was inside him. The love for his family, friends, his villagers, for the life itself and of course himself. In that way Amadeus could forgive himself for what he had done and live in harmony with the people around him. She also told the king that he should appreciate all the good things he had and if he learned from his mistakes, he would never commit another injustice.

Then Laura placed the key of *"**Trust**"* in his hands. With that key he could clear any doubts that existed in his heart. The power that the key had will be able to open the doors of "**Believe**"; meaning that everything is possible and that all his wishes would be come true if he has faith.

Finally, she gave him the key of *"**Gratitude**"*, this key would open the doors of knowledge, forgiveness and inner peace. When he feel grateful for all that he was, how little or much he had, for each sigh and every day lived. If he fell grateful despite the setbacks, failures, difficulties, betrayals, lies, and sorrows, the sky would be filled with joy and would let all its grace fall on him.

Laura's words fell deep into the heart of king Amadeus and everyone present in the great hall. They made them reflect on the value of people and the meaning of the small things that sometimes seem insignificant, but in reality they are the most important things in life. They also learned the true beauty, the one that goes beyond the visible, the one that it's found inside of each person, each being.

From that moment on everything changed, there were no differences among those present, it could be seen how the nobles embraced the plebeians, the princes, dukes, and princesses. All celebrated with the servants of the palace and other guests. Even Helios's heart of steel melted with so much love, he was so touched that he did not stop crying.

And so the royal banquet ended. The people from the neighboring kingdoms returned to their lands full of hope and peace. Zoe, Abigail, Laila, Felicidad, Catalina, and Esmeralda returned to their villages proudly bearing the royal shield.

On the other hand, Berarminia, Estephania, and Karmine began the trip back to their villages. However, they did not run with the same luck as the others, for not being worthy of the royal shield, since they only thought about their own interests and the profit of their families. Even so, King Amadeus agreed to help their villages thanks to Laura's intervention.

Laura was so noble that she never mentioned what Estephania, Karmine, and Berarminia had done to her. She forgave them and for that reason, she requested the King's favor for each of their villages. It was not fair for the other villagers to pay for the selfishness of them and their families.

Then the King ordered that a large furnace be built in the village of Pan de Frutas, so that all his villagers could work together to make fruit breads and other delicacies to be sold beyond their limits.

In the village of Monte Verde, the king ordered the construction of a fabric factory so that the neediest people could have a job and earn their livelihood. The fabrics will be sold at a low cost for the villagers of all Arabella so that they could afford a decently dress and not be ashamed of their old torn clothes.

To the village of Solgiral, King Amadeus ordered to expand its limits, for them to have more land to cultivate their plants. One of the cultivations was sunflowers which were not only beautiful but also possessed many properties like their seeds which could be used as food. The king had thought to extract their oils for consumption by the villagers of Arabella and thus all would be strong and healthy.

As for Ms. Clotilde, the king decided that she would no longer work as a tutor for the young ladies of Arabella; from that moment on, she would be in charge of taking care, bathing and feeding the animals in the stable. Therefore, Clotilde had to occupy the small room in the school where Laura slept. Fortunately for her, the room was clean and tidy thanks to Laura.

All this happened thanks to the clueless Esmeralda, who after obtained the royal shield, was able to recover from the nerves that came from being in front of the King. Esmeralda told Ms. Virginia and Ms. Rania everything that the ex-educator Clotilde planned with Karmine, Berarminia, and Estephania against Laura and that was the cause Laura was about to miss the royal banquet.

King Amadeus not only gave Laura the royal shield, he also named her the honorary princess of all Arabella. Laura was always very modest. She never wished to be a princess, or possess great wealth, so she rejected the title given by the King, but at the insistence of his words, she accepted it.

Amadeus wanted Laura to be known in all corners of the earth and to be remembered forever as the most beautiful princess of all, because her inner beauty was more important than her feature.

The King with great pride accompanied Laura on her journey back to Calabazas Village. He wanted to be reunited with his old friend Enrique. He also wanted to turn the small and humble village into the most prosperous of all Arabella. Amadeus had so many plans for Laura and for all of the villagers, who despite lacking material wealth, possessed the most valuable fortune of all, their "nobility". Laura was very happy, but before returning to Calabazas she had to say goodbye to someone very special...

On the way to her village, she asked King Amadeus to make a stop at the place where she met the wise Arkazú. She wants to thank him for his advice and of course for "***The three magic keys***". The King gladly pleased her; he also wanted to thank the old man for the precious gift.

When they arrived at the place, they found Arkazú resting under a leafy tree. Without Laura or the king saying a single word, Arkazú turned his gaze towards them and with a sweet smile told them that he was waiting for them because he knew they would come to see him.

_ "Before you both thank me for the keys, I want to tell you that it's not me that you have to thank. I'm just an instrument of God. Besides, the keys they are just objects like any other. They simply help you bring out the courage and power that each of you possess"...

_ "For example, if a person takes any stone and believes that it has special powers, then it will have it. Everything will depend on the faith the persons has in themselves and the intensity with which they want it," Arkazú continued.

The three magic keys

_ "The keys are made to open the doors of Love, Trust, and Gratitude as well as the doors of Grudge, Evil and Revenge. You have chosen to open the doors of good, while others have chosen to open the doors of evil".

_"Each person has the freedom to become light or darkness. Who chooses to be light will be happy despite the sorrows and difficulties that arise in their life and everyone around them will also would be happy, because the shared of good multiplies; but who chooses to be darkness can never be happy and will be condemned to live in solitude".

Suddenly, a whirlwind of light completely covered Arkazú, who gradually rose up to reach the clouds while Laura and king Amadeus were overflowing with happiness, from above the voice of the wise old man was heard:

"From now on, you will become the keys of all those people who have lost trust, love and hope, you will let them know that everything is possible when there is gratitude in their heart!".

King Amadeus and Laura were shaken with the words of Arkazú... They were no longer the same as before, now they were full of gratitude and wanted to share it with everyone, especially with the villagers of Calabazas…

Meanwhile, Benjamin as every afternoon climbed to the top of the mountain, hoping to see some sign of his daughter. That day he could not believe what he saw. A parade of carriages with the royal insignia was approaching, and among then he could see Molondrón!

Benjamin hurried down the mountain and along all the villagers to meet the King and Laura. The people were surprised to see Laura getting off the royal carriage with a tiara like the ones that princesses wore. Amadeus could not contain his excitement to see among the villagers his friend Enrique. Whom, he embraced effusively and unable to contain the tears, he told him how much he loved and missed him.

Enrique also responded very affected by the words of his friend. He always remembered the Majesty with great affection. Everyone in the village of Calabazas was very happy to see Laura again, her feature was the same, but she had a special brightness in her eyes, something had changed in her ... Laura now could see who she really was. She started to love and accepted herself which led her to be happier than before.

King Amadeus thanked all the villagers for being noble, honest and kind people. He told them about his plans to transform Calabazas into the most prosperous village of all Arabella and neighboring kingdoms. He also introduced Laura, as the new princess of the kingdom... "Princess Laura of Calabazas". That day king Amadeus celebrated with all the villagers of Calabazas his new rebirth.

Arkazu's words came true, both Laura and the King were responsible for spreading the words in *"The three magic keys"*: **LOVE**, **TRUST** and **GRATITUD**. All Arabella and the other kingdoms followed each of the wise advice provided by the keys and since then, all had a happy life living gratefully forever...

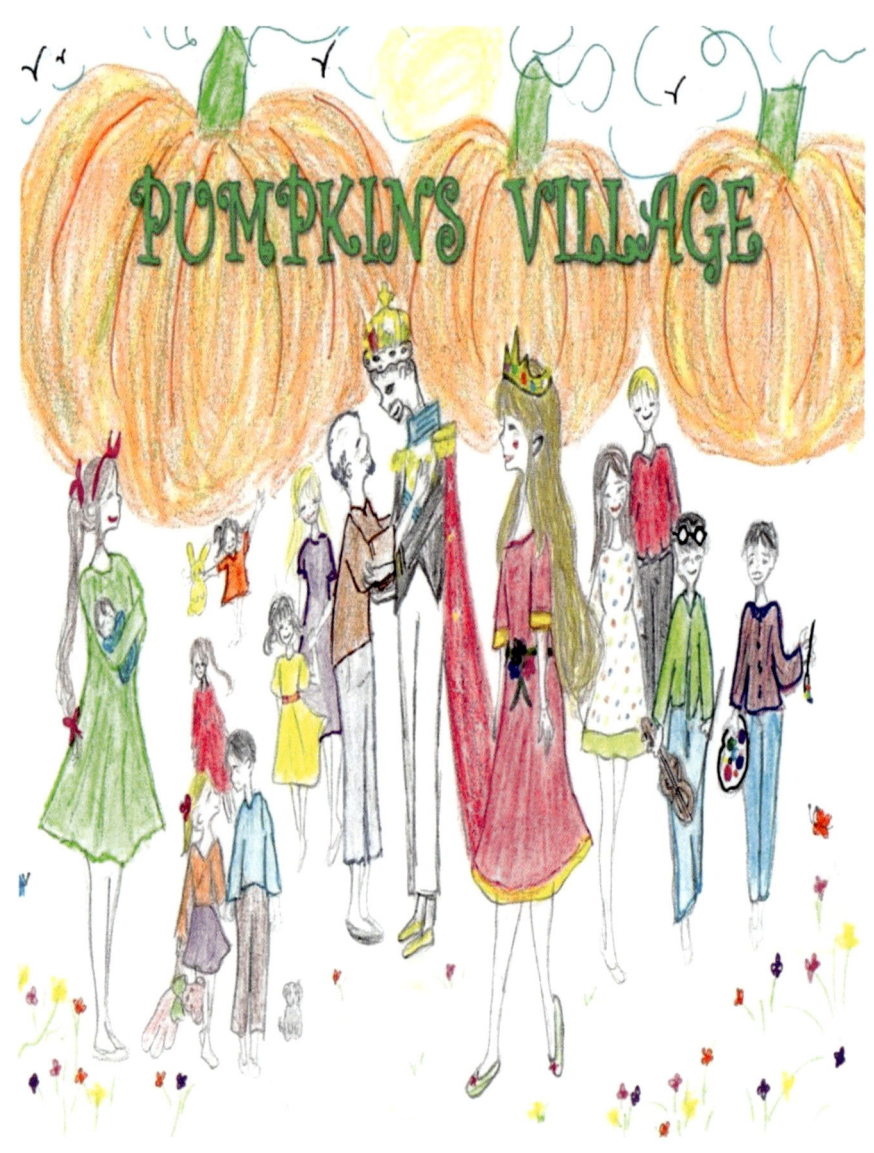

The three magic keys

Glossary

Calabazas	pumpkin
Flamboyán	It's one of the most colorful trees in the world for its red, orange, lilac flowers, and for its bright green foliage.
Los Lírios	The lilies flowers
Uveral	Name taken from the Spanish word "uva" wich mean grape
Carambolas	Star fruit
Champiñón	Mushroom
Solgiral	Name taken from the Spanish word "girasol" wich mean sunflower
Monte Verde	Green Mount
Pan de Frutas	Fruit bread
Damasco	Apricot fruit
Molondrón	It is a very nutritious vegetable that is also called okra.
Higüero	It is a tropical tree whose dried fruit was used by the Taínos to make pots and cups and nowadays they are used to make handicrafts.

Made in the USA
Monee, IL
06 January 2020